MAY . .. 2010

GET CRAFTY

AT THE SEASIDE

Vivienne Bolton

DP
DEMPSEY
PARR

Editor
Barbara Segall

Art Direction
Full Steam Ahead

DesignTeam
Design Study

Photography
Patrick Spillane

Photographic Co-ordinator
Liz Spillane

Styling
Bianca Boulton

Project Management
Kate Miles

The publishers would like to thank Inscribe Ltd., Bordon, Hants. for
providing the art materials used in these projects and
Sophie Boulton for her assistance.

First published in 1998 by
Dempsey Parr
13 Whiteladies Road, Clifton, Bristol
BS8 1PB

24681097531

Produced by Miles Kelly Publishing Ltd
Unit 11, Bardfield Centre, Great Bardfield, Essex CM7 4SL

British Library Cataloguing-in-Publication Data
A catalogue record for this book is available from the British Library.

ISBN 1-84084-194-X

Printed in Spain

GET CRAFTY

AT THE SEASIDE

Contents

DRIFTWOOD
Boats

When you go for a walk along the beach keep your eyes open for unusual items. This is called beachcombing. Driftwood is often washed up on the shore and collecting it is great fun, but what can you do with all those oddly shaped pieces of wood? Making small boats is one way of using them. The sails and flags can be cut from coloured tissue paper. You could make a miniature fleet of small craft and feature them on a sunny windowsill. You will need your imagination to create interesting boats, masts and sails. If you want to join pieces together, you will need to use a strong glue. Driftwood often looks good left a natural colour. However it sometimes needs decorating.

You will need:

Selection of driftwood pieces

Tissue paper

Sturdy scissors

Glue

Tissue paper

Paint

Paint-brush

Emery board

1 When making driftwood boats spend a lot of time planning the best use of particular pieces of wood you may have found. Occasionally you will find one that needs just a sail or a dot of paint to turn it into an interesting craft.

Sometimes you will need to change the shape of a piece of wood; strong scissors may do. Try using an emery board or a small piece of sandpaper to shape pieces to fit neatly together. Most of all you need to enjoy being creative with your seaside materials.

When beachcombing take care you do not injure yourself. Wear beachshoes and use rubber gloves. Check found items for nails and do not touch anything you don't recognize.

SHELLS AND DRIFTWOOD
Mobiles

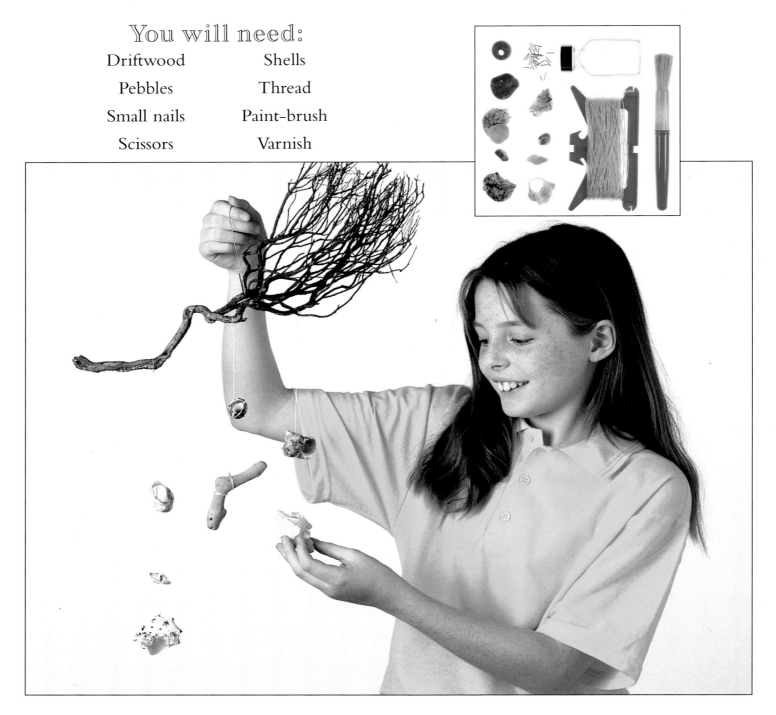

eachcombing can be very
rewarding: the tides wash all sorts of
things up on the beach. Interesting
pieces of water-smoothed driftwood and
pretty shells can be turned into mobiles and
hung up as a reminder of seaside days.
When making a mobile you need a shapely
piece of driftwood to start with. You can
use thread or string to tie on attractive
shells and stones. The mobile needs to be
well balanced. Check this by hanging the
mobile up as soon as you have a few pieces
tied on, adjusting the weight as you go.
Paint on a layer of varnish for a glossy look.

You will need:

Driftwood	Shells
Pebbles	Thread
Small nails	Paint-brush
Scissors	Varnish

1 You will need a piece of driftwood and some small nails to make the hanger for this mobile. Use a hammer to knock the nails into position.

2 Tie good knots when attaching the shells and driftwood to the string. Consider how the mobile will appear when hung up when you do this.

4 This mobile is made by tying the weighted strings directly onto the driftwood. You could use loops and hang the strings on or tie them on with small tight knots. You will need to check the mobile for balance as you make it. When the mobile is complete you might want to paint on a layer of varnish to give the shells a glossy finish.

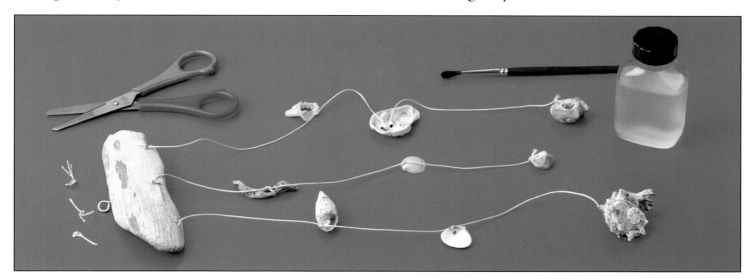

3 Once you are happy with the balance of the mobile, paint a layer of varnish onto the shells. Hang up your mobile and let it remind you of a very happy holiday.

Beach Shoes

Beach shoes are very useful, but usually come in rather dull black or white. Use fabric paints to decorate them. The fabric paints used in this project are available from craft and fabric shops and are easy to use. It is a good idea to practise first on a piece of card. Try out a few designs. Fish or flowers make good patterns. Choose a pattern that is easy to repeat.

You will need:

Canvas shoes

Fabric paint

Be sure to clean up any spills as they occur. Don't forget to leave your work area tidy.

1 These shoes have been painted with a seaside theme. Take care not to smudge the decoration as you go along. When you have completed the first shoe use it as a pattern for the other one. In that way you will be able to create a matching design. Once your shoes are decorated leave them in a safe place to dry completely before you wear them on your next beachcombing expedition.

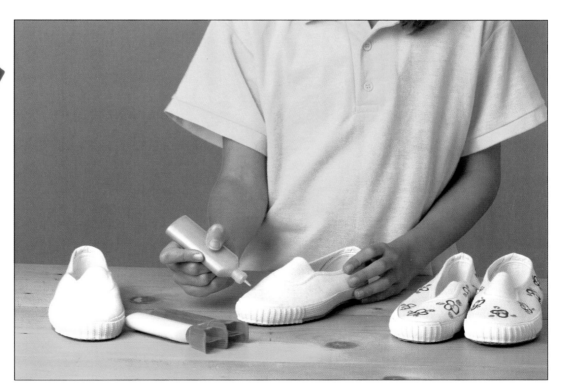

2 Flower patterns are easy to draw on and look very attractive. Decorate a pair of shoes to wear during the summer months. You could take inspiration from a special dress or T-shirt.

Lighthouse

Models are great fun to make. This lighthouse standing on a rocky island surrounded by the blue sea looks very realistic. Spend some time planning your model, then make a rough drawing. If you have been to the seaside you may recall a particular lighthouse or other seaside scene which you could re-create in miniature. When you are away on holiday you may want to collect a few pebbles and some sand to use to make the model when you return home. It is amazing what you can achieve with some plaster, pebbles and paint.

You will need:

A cardboard lid

Margarine tub

Stones

Pebbles

Plaster-of-Paris

Bowl and spatula

Air hardening clay

Glue

Paint and paint-brushes

1 Place the margarine tub towards one end of the box lid. Position the stones; they will jut out of the 'water' so need to be quite tall. When you are happy with the arrangement mix up the plaster-of-Paris in the bowl and pour it over everything.

2 You will now need to make the lighthouse. Use some air hardening clay and make a long cylinder shape, wider at one end than the other. The room at the top will need to be made separately. Leave the pieces to dry in a warm airy spot.

3 When the plaster and the lighthouse pieces are dry you can glue everything in place. Use strong glue. Leave the model in a warm airy spot to dry.

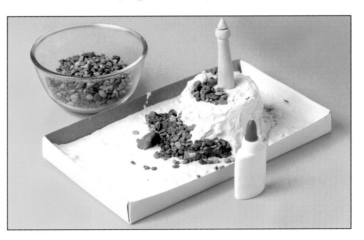

4 Spread a thick layer of glue where ever you need to place the small pebbles. These will give the impression of rocks. A few on top of the island will look good.

5 Once your model is dry it is ready to paint and decorate. Have fun and use plenty of imagination to create a realistic-looking rocky, seaside scene.

Photo Album

Seaside holidays are best remembered in photographs. Make one of these albums to keep your photographs safe. Choose bright nautical colours; blue and yellow are fun. The albums are made from card and coloured cord holds the pages together. Try making a seaside collage to decorate the cover. A beach scene or a gaily coloured yacht would look good.

You will need:

Thin coloured card

Coloured paper

Scissors

Hole punch

Cord

1 Cut the covers and pages to size. Use the hole punch to make holes through the covers and pages. You will need to take care that they line up. Thread coloured cord through the holes to hold the album together securely and tie a bow.

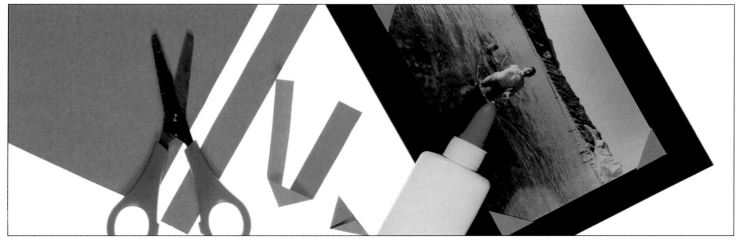

2 To make the photograph holders cut a narrow strip of paper. Fold the paper inwards to create a corner sleeve. Cut away any excess paper and glue the sleeve onto the page. Do this four times, one for each corner then insert the photograph.

3 Decorate the cover of your album with an attractive seaside collage. Use coloured paper to create this yacht and cut out a row of waves to glue along the bottom of the page.

Seaside Jewellery

S hells, attractive stones and small pieces of driftwood can be made up into earrings and pendants. Use fine wire and thread to assemble the jewellery. You can also buy ready-made clasps and earring backs from craft shops. These are called jewellery findings. Look along the seashore for two matching shells with small holes in and make them up into earrings. As you walk along the beach keep an eye out for interestingly shaped, coloured stones.

You will need:

Pebbles and shells

Wire

Thread

Jewellery findings

Varnish

Paint-brush

1 These dainty shell earrings are easy to make. These shells have tiny holes naturally occurring in them. However you may have to use a press-together jewellery binding to hold the shell in place. Attach the earring hook to each shell and you have a pretty pair of earrings to wear as a reminder of your seaside visit.

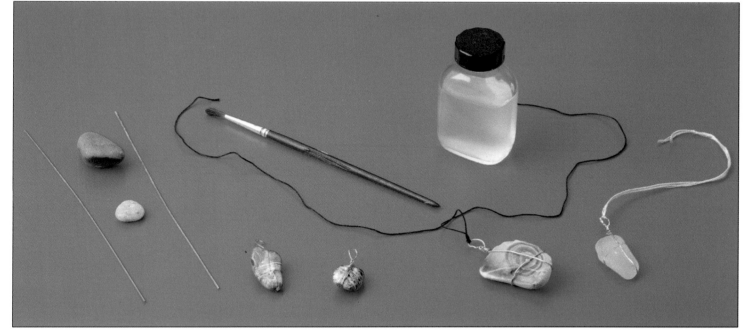

2 To make these pendants you will need some attractively marked pebbles. Use clear varnish painted over the pebbles to bring out the rich patterns (clear nail varnish works just as well). Wind a piece of wire around the pebble and finish with a loop at the top. Attach a piece of thread to the loop and use this to hang your pendant around your neck.

Check that it is okay to pick up shells along the beach where you are.

Three-in-a-row

Three-in-a-row is a good game to both make and to play. Once you have made a board you can make a selection of counters, different sets to suit different occasions. The boards are made from card and craft wood while the counters are made from oven bake clay.

Matching shells make good counters too. To play the game you need two players. Each player takes turns placing a counter on the board. You must both try to take defensive action when it's your turn, to prevent the other player from getting three-in-a-row. The first player to get a row wins.

You will need:

Thick coloured card

Craft strip-wood

Scissors

Paint-brush

Oven bake clay

Shells

Glue

1 Begin by painting the craft strip-wood in your chosen colour. Choose a colour that co-ordinates with the thick coloured card you will use for the base of the board. Leave it until it is thoroughly dry.

3 Attach the sides to the board with glue. Cut the board markings from thin strip-wood and glue these in place. Make sure you position them correctly on the board.

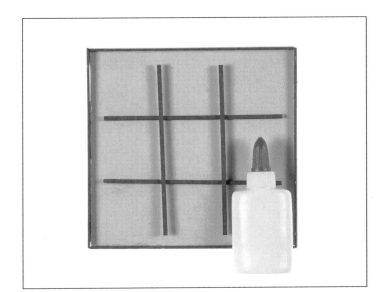

2 The size of your games board is decided by the piece of thick coloured card. This will need to be square. Cut the sides for your board to length from the craft strip-wood, using your board as a pattern.

4 Glue on the cross markings. Don't worry if your paintwork gets a little scratched. Once the glue is dry you can use paint to touch up any spots that might need it.

5 These noughts and crosses counters are made from oven bake clay. Use different colours and check that the counters fit the available space on the board. Try your hand at making little boats, dolphins and starfish as a variation from flat counters.

Paperweights

Pebble painting is fun and a good rainy day activity. Collect pebbles along the beach and save them. When you want to enjoy a quiet time get out the paints and your imagination, and make these attractive paperweights. You could paint a tiny row of pebble cottages (use a fine paint-brush to paint on tiny windows and doors) and little rose bushes along the cottage front. Or try your hand at painting a tiny kitten on a pebble or a fish or even a skeleton.

1 These interesting decorations need a little time and practice. Wash and dry the pebbles before you begin. Use a fine paint-brush to paint in the detail. Once you are happy with your chosen decoration and the paint has dried, add a layer of varnish.

2 A row of painted pebble cottages makes a good ornamental display. Choose pebbles which have suitable shapes and which can stand up. You may need to apply two coats of paint to the house and roof to give a good surface for decorating. When you have painted the cottages give them a coat of varnish to protect them and to give them a glossy finish.

You will need:
Pebbles

Paint, varnish and paint-brushes

Tablemats

Mosaics are usually created using small square tiles. To make these tablemats we have cut lots of small squares from paper and used them glued onto sugar paper to create a fishy picture. Choose bright colours to create your pictures. Squares cut from magazine pictures can also be used to make mosaics. The important thing to remember, when making a mosaic, is to keep the lines straight. This gives the impression of tiles all lined up. Use a ruler and pencil to make markings on your paper so that you can keep the squares neat and in order.

You will need:

Paper

Ruler

Pencil

Scissors

Glue

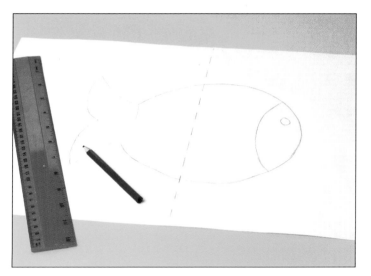

1 Begin by drawing a simple outline of a fish on your paper. Make sure that the picture is centrally placed.

2 Use the ruler and pencil to measure out squares and cut them out in your chosen colours. You will need a lot of squares.

3 Glue on the squares. Begin in a corner of the picture and try to work from one side of the picture to the other.

4 Your finished fish mosaic should look something like this. You could make a set of table mats for the family.

5 For a special event you might want to decorate some table napkins to match your table mats. Use paper and create pretty collage pictures.

Flowerpots

Flowerpots look good sitting along a sunny windowsill. Fill them with brightly coloured flowers to bring a little of the garden indoors. These pots are decorated with shells bought from a specialist craft shop. The shells are all recycled. The creatures that used to live in them are used as food in some countries and the shells simply thrown away. Ask at your local craft shops for them. If you gather them yourself, always check that you are allowed to on that particular beach.

You will need:

Shells

Terracotta pot or container to recycle

Grout

Spatula

Paint

Paint-brush

Glue

Varnish

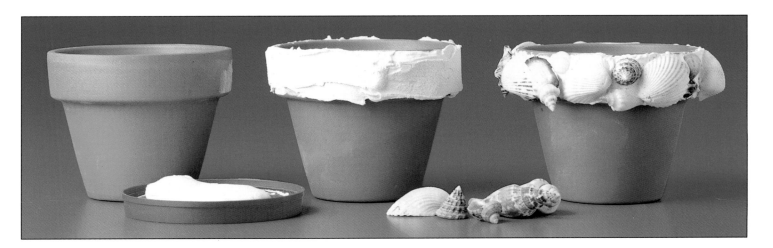

1 Choose your plant pot and shells. Use a spatula to apply a layer of grout along the rim of the pot. Press the shells firmly into the grout. Leave the grout to dry. When it is dry you may want to apply a little varnish to bring out the colours of the shells.

2 These pretty pink pots have been decorated with tiny shells. Begin by painting the pot pink. You may need two coats of paint. After the paint is dry use strong glue to attach the shells. When the glue has set apply a layer of varnish to the shells.

CARD AND GLITTER
Aquarium

The fish floating in this model aquarium are made from thin card and decorated with paint and glitter. They shimmer through the weed and clear blue sea very realistically when you gently shake the box. Use a large shoe box to make the aquarium. You could make a shoal of tiny fish to weave their way through the weed. The fish are suspended from the ceiling of the box with thin gold thread which is almost invisible. Place a few rocks and shells in the bottom of the box. If you have one, a model shipwreck would make an attractive feature.

You will need:
Large shoebox

Scissors

Paint & paint-brush

Blue plastic film

Tissue paper

Thin card and paper

Felt tip pens

Glue

Glitter

Gold thread

Pebbles

1 Cut a rectangle from the box lid.

2 Cut a rectangle from the base of the box.

3 Paint the box and lid blue, inside and out.

4 Glue blue film over the cut-out spaces.

5 Cut strips of tissue paper for weeds. Glue them in place suspended from the roof of the aquarium. Use two colours of green.

6 Draw fish on the thin card and decorate them with paint and glitter. Attach them to the lid of the box with gold thread.

Fishing Game

Fishing games always go down well at parties and games evenings. This fishing game is quite easy to make. The fish hooks and the fish mouths are made from paper clips. You could also make fish in two colours or make several different sea creatures, such as fish and starfish. Then players can see how many of each they can 'catch' in a given time. Another game might be to give each fish a value, adding the values at the end of the game to see which 'catch' is worth the most. This would introduce gamesmanship as each player goes for the highest value catch.

You will need:

Plate

Thick card

Thin card

Scissors

Glue

Sticky tape

Ruler

Felt tips

Sticks

String

Paper clips

1 Use a plate as an outline for a circular shape on a piece of thick card. Cut out the circle. This will be the base of the pond. Measure out a long strip of thin card for the sides. Tape it to the base.

2 The sides of the pond will prevent the fish from jumping out! Use coloured tape or felt tip pens to decorate the sides.

3 Draw the fish and starfish on a piece of thick card and decorate them using felt tip pens. Cut them out. You will need to make quite a few fish and starfish.

4 Now make the loops on the decorated stars and fish from paper clips. You will need to fold up a section of the paper clip and attach it with sticky tape to the fish and starfish.

5 The fishing rods are made from garden sticks. Tie a piece of string to one end of each stick and a paper clip to the end of each piece of string. Shape the paper clip into a hook.

Lettercards

Making lettercards is easy, fun and turns letterwriting into a creative activity. Make these lettercards before you set off on your seaside holiday. Then you will have a supply to send to friends from your holiday home. Decorate your lettercards with flowers, fish, tiny boats or other seaside scenes. You will need a large dinner plate to draw around. Once your lettercard is decorated and written you can fold it up ready to post as it turns into its own envelope. Lettercards are good for writing thank you letters or short wish-you-were-here notes while you are on holiday. A set of decorated lettercards would make a good gift.

You will need:

Paper

Plate

Colouring pencils

Small rectangular box

Stickers

1 Place the plate on the sheet of white paper and use it to draw a circle.

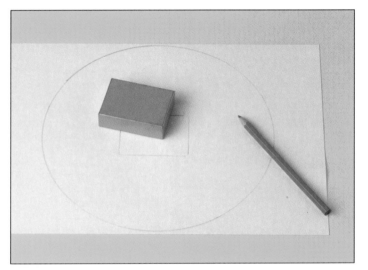

2 Place the small rectangular box in the centre of the circle and draw around it. This will be the address label.

3 Use scissors to cut out the circle. Your lettercard is now ready to decorate. You need to decorate around the address label.

4 The pattern on this lettercard is decorated in seaside colours of blue and yellow.

5 Turn the lettercard over to the blank side This is where you will write your letter. Rule lines to write on.

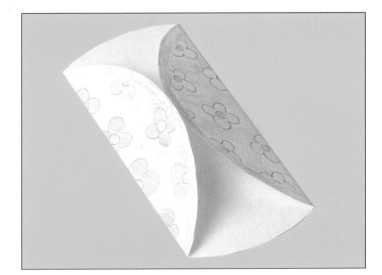

6 When you have written your letter, fold the sides inward and use a sticker to hold the lettercard closed.

Treasure Boxes

Shells can be used decoratively in so many ways. In this project they are used to decorate a small storage box and to make a pretty circular picture frame. You will need an empty cheese box and some shells to make the storage box plus some grout or strong glue to attach the shells. You can arrange them in a regular pattern or randomly over the lid. The picture frame is made from thin card.

You will need:

Empty cheese box

Selection of shells

Grout

Spatula

Thin card

Scissors

Varnish

Paint-brush

If you do not have any grout you could use some strong glue.

1 First check that the box is clean. Before you begin, experiment with the design. Lay the shells on the lid without any grout. When you are happy with the design spread a layer of grout across the box lid using the spatula and gently press the shells in place.

3 To make this pretty shell encrusted picture frame you will need a circle of thin card with a hole cut out of the centre. This will make the frame shape. Apply a layer of grout using the spatula and gently press the shells into an attractive pattern around the edge.

2 Leave the box in a warm airy spot to dry. You will need to give the shell covered box plenty of time to dry off. When it is dry paint on a layer of varnish to give the shells an attractive finish.

4 When the grout has dried the frame is ready for a layer of varnish. This will protect it and bring out the colours. Now you can insert a photograph and hang up the frame or use it as a small paperweight.

Index